She's Awakened From Pain to Purpose

Her Truth. Her Experience. God's Grace.

Julia J Banks

She's Awakened From Pain to Purpose

Unless otherwise noted, scriptures were taken from the Holy Bible, King James Version (KJV), Copyright© 1996.

Paperback ISBN: 978–1-735-63033-5

Printed and bound in the United States of America

Book Designed by Brand It Beautifully™

www.branditbeautifully.com

DEDICATION

To my niece, Takeitha Banks:

You had to sacrifice time we would have spent together so that I could finish this project.

Thank you. I appreciate and love you always.

Contents

Acknowledgments

To Ally Chiniski, Brandiez Saimone, Domonique Jefferson, Holly Noble, Kelly Brown Elie, Peyton Johnson Harrison, Teron Hughes and Zanyah Banks. Some of you went places emotionally that allowed you to be vulnerable in a way that I know will speak to our readers. Thank you all for being a part of this process and trusting me with your story. I am looking forward to seeing what you produce as well in your future endeavors.

To Allison Denise of Brand It Beautifully™, your patience, guidance, and professionalism is what helped this come into fruition. Thank you.

To my mother, whom I miss dearly, for all of your love and support you always push me to be all that God has called me to be. Thank you.

PREFACE

In the pages of this book you will find women from various walks of life, each with their own story, some may be similar but told in a very unique way that is specific to them. See it doesn't matter how many people have the same story we all have different experiences that we view in different ways and we will tell it from that point of view.

This anthology was written by women to share their pain and how God brought them to a place of purpose. You will read stories of domestic violence, childhood trauma, sickness, mental illness, death, and abandonment. These stories will also show you that despite what you have experienced you can overcome it.

-She's Awakened Anthology

INTRODUCTION

"We all have a story. We all have experiences that we can share to empower, encourage, and inspire someone. What we don't all have is the willingness to share the truth of it. We tend to want to dress it up and make it look nice and cute so we can put it on a shelf for the guest to see and feel proud but whose story is really like that. If we're honest with ourselves no one's story truly is.

She's Awakened From Pain To Purpose is a collection of women's stories. These women, although they have come from various walks of life all have one thing in common. That one thing is their story. It's one of pain and disappointment, one of trauma and loss but also one of victory over defeat. Their lived and now shared experiences are now being told to us in an attempt to offer hope and encouragement to those who read it.

These women told their stories and spoke their truth from an authentic place, not to impress but to empower, so that you would know that you too have the ability to awaken from the pain of your past and walk in the power of your purpose."

-Julia

GRIEF
A POEM BY
ZANYAH BANKS

GRIEF IS REAL AND WHEN IT HITS IT LEAVES YOU standing still

You're left wondering, how could this be?

Like, we was just on the phone, nah, I gotta see

Cause see, first you in denial, like nope, this can't be real

Keep going over it in your head like, "that just wasn't the deal"

They gotta be home, please just pick up the phone

They can't be gone, they was just way too strong

And then suddenly anger hit

You mad at the world and don't give a damn about it

Screaming it's your fault, it's your fault – or maybe it's mine.

Ready to fight any and everybody who says it's gonna be fine

Because to you, it's not

Your heart is shattered and the pain won't stop

All you can say is, "God I would give anything to have them back

I promise I won't quit, I won't slack

But if I could see their face just one mo' time

Then I know everything will be just fine"

And then the tears start to fall

You're convinced you have no one to call

You're crying and questioning how to say goodbye

You weren't prepared for them to fly high.

Sometimes I wake up like Biggie and say,

"It was all a dream" – then reality hit, it's more like a nightmare.

But I'll get through this,

I know your presence is still here.

In the Midst of Pain

Inspired by Donald Ray Jefferson Sr.

Domonique Jefferson

My name is Domonique and I would like to take you on a journey through the life of my late husband. Donald was pure fun, joy, and light in our home. My husband was my best friend, the priest of our home, a listener and friend to many, and full of love and compassion. Donald did some writing and wrote a short autobiography. This is Donald, in his own words:

"My name is Donald Ray Jefferson, and I am the "knee" baby in my family. I am the last son born and the next to last child born of 11 children. My relationship with my siblings was great. We worked on our "farm" and played together well. I grew up in a small, spread-out country, simple and peaceful-back then, town. I grew up in Henderson, Nc. My best childhood memory was going fishing, and then cooking the fish by the lake on a fire with my dogs protecting me. As a child we went to church every Sunday. During young adulthood I went to church on holidays. I rededicated my life to Christ in 2008 or 2009. I have gone through being a "baby" Christian, "adolescent" and "teenage" Christian and now have a firm relationship with God. My spirituality guides my day-to-day life completely. I pray for every decision I make. I was in the United States army from Feb 85'- March 2008. I then took a short retirement and I currently work for the American Red Cross. I feel good about my job now. It is like I am still serving because I work with the military. I get to help people out and have the opportunity to minister. I have an outstanding relationship with my coworkers and boss. I plan to stay with the red cross until retirement."

— (Excerpt taken from Donald's Autobiography, written August 5, 2019, 6:34pm)

Donald did "retire" from the Red Cross, but it wasn't how either of us expected. Here begins a story of overcoming by the blood of the lamb and the word of our testimony (see Revelation 12:11). Picture a beautiful day in October of 2019. Donald and I were dressed up. I was in a yellow sundress and Donald was in jeans with a pressed, blue-collared shirt. The children had dressed up as well as we posed for a picture. Our daughter held a sign that said, "We're Adopting!" The photographer said, "Smile!" We smiled our biggest, most hopeful, all-is-right-in-the-world smiles and a photograph memorialized that day in history. Just like the sign said, we were hoping to adopt. All of the background checks, physicals, psychological, educational, and financial documents were complete. Our last step in the process was getting professional photographs taken for the book that would describe our family to expecting mothers thinking of placing their child up for adoption. Donald and I were excited to see the baby that would be joining our family. We had been praying together as a couple and family for God to add to our family – and it was finally happening! During his physical for the adoption, Donald told the doctor he had upper right-side abdominal pain. The doctor thought that, since Donald was an avid weightlifter, he had pulled a muscle. Donald rested but the pain lingered. My husband decided to go back to the doctor for the pain. The doctor recommended a CT scan and said he would call and give the results over the phone. A few days later, a nurse called and asked my husband what day he could come in so the doctor could speak with him about the results. The nurse told him the doctor didn't want to discuss it over the phone. As a family, we began to pray about this concerning turn of events. We found that Philippians 4:7 "And the peace of God, which transcends all understanding, will guard your hearts and your minds in Christ Jesus" gave us the peace we needed in the days leading up to the appointment.

The appointment came and the doctor, who was a family care physician, had never seen anything like what was on the scan. The doctor thought Donald might have a liver worm from sloshing through the jungles as a young man in the Army. The doctor didn't think that the scan was revealing cancer and the blood work report indicated no cancer. We were happy to hear this news, but a follow up appointment with a liver specialist in Oklahoma City was necessary. We thought we were in for a long wait and were shocked when the phone rang the very next day. The Cancer Center in Oklahoma City would see us in two days. What unfolded at that appointment was like swallowing pure bitterness, a forest fire to our dreams. Our plans came crashing down in one appointment. Donald didn't have a liver worm, he had cholangiocarcinoma or bile duct liver cancer. This cancer was rare and only 1 in 100,000 people battled it. My stomach dropped, my mind raced, and questions began to flow out of me quickly for the doctor to answer. My husband, who was the most talkative person I knew, couldn't speak a word. Later, Donald would tell me that his body was in the room, but his mind departed from the shock. We left the room to go to our car and Donald said, "Let's go to the courtyard." The courtyard was beautiful; it had a towering fountain and large, lush, tropical plants. Donald walked around smiling, radiating his trust in God. We even snapped a picture. His smile was genuine and so was his happiness, despite the news he had just received. He never missed a moment to enjoy life with a smile on his face.

Donald was a praying man. When I met Donald, we weren't living a life of following Christ. I knew I wasn't where I needed to be, so I refused to pray. I felt like it would be better for me if God just left me, because I felt I wasn't good enough to be loved. Donald, on the other hand, would pray daily. He said his mother, Cleo, taught him to pray. No matter where he was in life, Donald would pray. I would watch him many nights, then one night I got down on my knees beside him out of respect – until I realized that if I was down there, I may as well pray too. This lesson in praying was the first and most powerful lesson Donald taught me. "Let your gentleness be evident to all. The Lord is near, Do not be anxious about anything, but in every situation, by prayer and petition, with thanksgiving, present your requests to God. And the peace of God, which transcends all understanding, will guard your hearts and your minds in Christ Jesus." Philippians 4:5-7.

Things went fast after the diagnosis. Donald received the diagnosis on a Friday and had liver resection surgery on Tuesday. The tumor was the size of a grapefruit and the cause of Donald's pain. The surgery took over six hours to complete. Donald was in a lot of pain but, "Walking was required to get out of the hospital," as he put it. On the worst day of his pain, with an IV pole in hand and a tube hanging out of his side, I was walking with Donald and helping him to brace against the handrails when we saw a young lady up ahead of us. This young lady was crying and, being the compassionate people-person he was, Donald, though in pain, wanted to stop to see if we could help. The lady was crying outside of the intensive care unit door because her brother was inside. Her brother was a teenager and had been struck by a pickup truck while mowing grass on a tractor. The doctors didn't think the boy would make it but his sister wanted to go in, lay hands on him, and pray. Donald, with all of the strength he had, stood up straight and told her "Let's pray." We stood in that hallway, praying and declaring God's word over this woman so that she would have the courage to go in and pray for her brother. In that moment, I saw a different side of my husband. While prayer was what he did in ministry, seeing him do it in a state of pain and suffering was new. I didn't know that I would continue to see Donald modeling how to suffer well for the next almost 3 years. "And the God of all grace, who called you to his eternal glory in Christ, after you have suffered a little while, will himself restore you and make you strong, firm and steadfast." 1 Peter 5:10.

My husband would continue to battle cancer, enduring a battery of chemotherapy and radiation. The chemotherapy left Donald itchy, but he would work out through the uncomfortable side effect with his exercise bands and a smile. A brief remission came but the cancer returned after a 3-month break and Donald would endure two different types of trial drugs. The drugs would deplete his body and he would need blood transfusions. As soon as the blood transfusion gave him enough energy, I would find Donald working out in his weight room and listening to the Bible App. Donald had listened to and studied the bible cover to cover many times. The word of God and prayer were his firm foundations.

Donald and I received so much bad news, but the joy of the Lord was our strength. At some point, Donald started double winking at me during appointments when the news was disheartening. His code double wink was simply closing your eyes toward each other tightly twice, but it communicated "I am here, I love you, God will see us, through." Donald was a well-practiced soldier in God's army. Although he was sick, he continued to serve pouring out to his family, friends, and community; 2 Timothy 4:6 "or I am already being poured out like a drink offering, and the time for my departure is near." We prayed fervently and believed that cancer would not cause Donald's death – and God was faithful. Cancer did not cause Donald's death. Donald Ray Jefferson Sr. died on April 3, 2022, of a massive brain bleed resulting from a stroke. Cancer did not win; Donald was taken to heaven on God's timetable. The last lesson Donald taught me was to believe God and keep serving until we go to our heavenly home. Three days before Donald passed, he was still fulfilling his purpose in pain. While sitting on his hospital bed before discharge, he had an audience of four men in his VA hospital room. Donald, although his body was depleted, was giving wisdom and encouragement through gospel to his roommates before he was to be discharged. On the day of his transition from earth to heaven though he could not speak or open his eyes to wink even though the doctors said it was not possible - Donald was double squeezing my hand reminding me God would see us through.

My husband, Donald Ray Jefferson Sr., taught me that pain and suffering cannot stop you from having love and compassion. The pain we endured together could not compare to the glory God was receiving as Donald fulfilled his purpose in pain. The pain I have while grieving my husband will also not be comparable to the joy that is coming as I fulfill my purpose. Pain is just a part of the purpose process; I can see that clearly now. Sometimes pain pushes us into purpose and other times we walk out our purpose in the midst of pain. Thank you, Donald Ray Jefferson Sr., for discipling me.

Revelation 12:11 "They triumphed over him by the blood of the Lamb and by the word of their testimony; they did not love their lives so much as to shrink from death."

Meet the Author

Domonique is the widow of the late Donald Ray Jefferson Sr. She is a mother to three biological children, Asaiah, Elijah, and Abrielle, and two bonus sons, Donald Jr. and Terence. She is a lover of farm animals, dogs, cats, and parakeets. Domonique specializes in raised bed gardening and the hügelkultur technique. Domonique is a minister of the gospel whenever and wherever she is called and hopes to impact the lives of additional foster youth in the near future. Domonique Nicole Jefferson holds a Bachelor of Arts in Christian Studies with an Emphasis in Biblical Studies from Grand Canyon University. Domonique is unashamed of the gospel of Jesus Christ, as it is the power of God that brings salvation to everyone who believes.

Connect with her:

Dnikj09@yahoo.com

She Lived Through It, So Can You!

Kelly Brown - Elie

This is not just my story. This story is mainly about my late mother and how God used her pain for purpose, from my perspective. My mother, Virginia Hamilton, gained her wings and transitioned from labor to reward on February 22, 2022, two days before my birthday. Our world will never be the same, but the life lessons and insights she taught my family will last a lifetime. I believe my mom's purpose was to show us how to live and serve God regardless of our circumstances, illnesses, and pain. I pray my mother's testimony helps bring people to Jesus, while teaching how we can overcome life's challenges by changing how we choose to react and respond to the circumstances in our lives. I pray her testimony takes root and bears fruit in your life as you read her story.

Virginia Ann Brown was born on a cold fall day, November 22, 1957, to the late Lloyd and Lucille Brown. She was one of six children who, together, made many long-lasting memories. Along with her siblings, cousins, and friends, she experienced a fun-filled and exciting life growing up in Vienna, VA. Mom's life wasn't easy, but it was filled with love and unspeakable joy. She didn't grow up having much but her parents made sure all their children knew and felt how much they were loved. Her family home was full of laughter and good memories. She grew up in Northern Virginia and lived in a very family-oriented community, where most of her neighbors were relatives. Mom was very close to her parents and her siblings, but her brother Lloyd (also known as Bubble) was her best friend.

Mom was a tomboy growing up, ditching dolls for toy guns and GI Joes. She often used to tell us this story of how her and her only brother, Bubble, were known as the bad kids on the hill. Those two would get into all kinds of trouble together; throwing rotten tomatoes or rocks at the neighborhood kids that were mean to them. She would say, "Those kids would get so mad and try to catch Bubble and I, but we were too fast for them." Wherever Bubble went, Mom wasn't far behind. This bond continued into adulthood, until Bubble passed away due to pneumonia at the young age of 28.

Mom was sickly growing up, finding out at age 17 that she had type 1 diabetes and having to take insulin injections for most of her life to manage her blood sugar. At the age of 19 she found out she was born with one kidney. She was hit with one illness after the other over the years. She would have month-long stays in the hospital during pregnancies, a double organ transplant, a hysterectomy that almost took her life, and her first heart attack at the age of 39. She was also diagnosed with cardiomyopathy, congestive heart failure, and COPD [chronic obstructive pulmonary disease]. June 2, 1999 was one of the hardest days of my life. I was 16 years old and worried sick about my best friend, my hero, my confidant, my mother. Sitting in the family waiting room at Fairfax Hospital with the rest of my family seemed like an eternity.

She was about to go under the knife and endure a double transplant: kidney and pancreas. As I sat there, waiting for twelve of the longest hours ever, all I kept thinking was, "Please, God, do not let her die. I will do anything, please just heal her, she can't die, please." I begged and pleaded with God. I told God that if He would heal my mom, I would serve Him all of the days of my life. I cried and had angry conversations with God in my head. But, in my heart, I knew her only hope was God and God alone. I guess I will now interject and tell you how Mom ended up on the operating table at Fairfax Hospital to begin with.

She married the love of her life, Wallace Hamilton, and had four beautiful children and two bonus daughters. She has four grandchildren. About a year before June 1999, while working at a nursing home in Manassas, VA, Mom's health started to deteriorate. In a matter of months, we were told she was in kidney failure and would need a transplant if she was going to live. Additionally, the diabetes was having the same effect on her pancreas. What!? Organ failures... transplant to live? This all seemed foreign and like a nightmare to me. I wasn't sure what was going to happen to my mom, but I had recently become a child of God. I had said the sinner's prayer and accepted Jesus Christ as my personal Lord and Savior, so I knew that God was indeed her only hope of beating this. I was an active member of Souls Harbor Church of God. I participated in the Youth Group, Youth Choir, and Sunday morning worship. I had everyone I knew praying for my mom and her healing.

Mom started dialysis and was put on the National Kidney Foundations Transplant List for eleven months before she received her kidney. During this time, it was a struggle to watch my vibrant, always-on-the-go Mom, turn into a weak, very sick woman. Our family had no idea how her surgery would change our lives. The things Mom used to love to do, like shopping, working, and hosting family functions, were much harder for her to manage. Daily tasks like cooking and cleaning became hard, but she still managed to cook daily meals for our family and continued cooking those meals for her husband after we left home. I hated seeing her sick and I always wanted to be with her. I would even skip school to go to her doctor's appointments with her. It felt like someone had turned our entire world upside down within a blink of an eye. Her life was in jeopardy and I felt helpless.

The day of her transplant, we waited for the doctors to come out with news about how the surgery went and how she was doing. Anxiously, we tried to make small talk and play games, but nothing we did could distract us from the fact that Mom's life hung in the balance and there was nothing we could do about it. I sat in silence, patiently waiting until I finally fell asleep. I woke up to doctors saying her surgery was a success. Her body was accepting both organs. The doctor proceeded to tell my family that the donor of her organs was a young African American, around age 20, that was such a match for her he could have been her son. We were so sad that a family had lost their son at the beginning of his life but so grateful that he chose to be an organ donor and saved our mom's life. As the doctor was talking, in a moment of joy, I screamed out, "That's all God."

As the years progressed and I graduated from high school, college, and seminary, Mom's health continued to decline. There were highs and lows throughout the years. Some years were better for her than others, but she made it through. Her faith in God was her greatest sense of comfort and strength. She leaned on God when nothing else would work and God carried her through. Have you had the privilege to know and walk alongside a living angel? Most people would probably say "no," so don't feel bad if you're one of them. I was blessed enough to have a real-life angel as my mother – someone who strived to live her life as closely to Jesus as was possible for a sinner saved by grace through faith. This doesn't mean my mom was perfect, as she wasn't in fact Jesus. However, she embodied Jesus' spirit as best she could. Forgiveness was second nature to my mom. No one was a stranger to her. She would literally give you the clothes on her back and her last dollar if you needed it.

My Mom was a classy, sassy lady. She loved to get dressed up. Anytime she left the house, she looked good. She loved fixing her makeup and getting her hair and nails done. She loved jewelry and sold Avon products for years. She absolutely loved to shop. Dollar General, Walmart, and Rainbow were a few of her favorites. Mom would often get fixed up in the evenings, right before my dad came home from work, so he would see her looking flawless even though she was in constant pain. She loved seeing the smile on his face when he came home.

Mom greeted everyone with, "How you doing?" This phrase embodied my mom. She was always concerned with how others were feeling. It brought her joy to be the listening ear for her family and friends. Mom would always ask you how you were doing instead of talking about her daily ailments, illnesses, and pain. Being the matriarch of our family, she was the glue that kept us all together. She was in constant communication with the family. She loved calling us on birthdays and sending cards for all occasions. She loved family gatherings. She didn't let her illnesses or pain keep her from enjoying life and spending quality time with those she loved most. She enjoyed cookouts and was famous for her macaroni salad, BBQ chicken wings, green beans, and chitterlings at Thanksgiving and Christmas. She was the life of the party and made everyone feel welcomed and at home.

Mom's legacy is rich in love, patience, kindness, forgiveness, resilience, and favor. Even on her deathbed, she was mothering her children and worrying about how her husband, children, and grandchildren would cope with her transition. If you take anything from my mom's story, my hope would be that you see the hand of God throughout life. God used her pain for purpose. She did not let her health challenges stop her from living, serving God, or loving those with whom she came in contact. It is because of her faith and love of Christ that I am who I am today. It is because of her selflessness that so many were touched by her life – even those who have come to know Jesus because of her. I am so grateful to have loved and been loved by an angel among us.

It's hard for me to put into words how my mom's journey has affected me. To watch someone you love more than life itself go through so much for so long is gut-wrenching. If I can be honest, at times I was angry with God for allowing one of his best to continuously struggle with health challenges, year after year. But through my mom's life, I learned and saw first-hand God's provision every step of the way. I have learned resilience and faith from my mom. She showed me what it's like to go through trials with grace. I am who I am in Christ because my mom's faith never wavered. Unfortunately, I deal with some of the same illnesses and struggles my mom faced. I am able to get through my own pain, with purpose because I know I'm not alone; what I'm going through is a part of my own testimony.

My mom always wanted to write a book as her testimony to the goodness of God and how He brought her through. Unfortunately, she didn't get the chance to tell her story, but I am so honored to share her journey with the world through my lens. Mom touched death's door many times throughout her life, but God always healed her. When she got sick this time, we thought she would make it through like all the other times before. But this was her time to go. She fought the good fight of faith and was met at the pearly gates with arms outstretched and hearing "Well done, my good and faithful servant." Through my mom's life, God was able to use her pain to show His mercy and grace. He used her illnesses to shine light on God's goodness. She showed us what it's like to keep the faith even when the odds are stacked against you. Her story is one of hope, faith, and strength. I know that she is beyond proud. Rest easy in heaven, Mom. This isn't goodbye but see you later. I love you now and forever.

MEET THE AUTHOR

Kelly Brown-Elie was born and raised in Northern Virginia. Kelly considers her faith and family to be most important in her life. She is a child of God, wife, mother, pastor, writer, poet, and friend. Kelly has devoted her life to God in true worship and desires to be used to motivate, inspire, and arouse the body of Christ to worship God in spirit and in truth. Minister Brown-Elie graduated from Bridgewater College in 2005, double majoring in sociology and religion and philosophy. She graduated from Wesley Theological Seminary in 2009 with her Master of Divinity. She is pursuing ordination in the United Methodist Church and looks forward to what God has for her life and ministry. She is an avid reader and writer and loves journaling daily. This first-time author counts it all a joy to be used in such a time as this!

CONNECT WITH HER:

Kelly.brownelie@gmail.com

www.facebook.com/kelly.brownelie

SILENCE
A POEM BY
ZANYAH BANKS

WHAT DO YOU EQUATE SILENCE TO BE?

Silence equals violence for me

Cause when I'm silent,

It's the only time I see

The true pain and hurt that dwell inside of me

Sitting in the corner,

With my knees to chest and my head to knees

Tears rolling as my insides scream, Lord, help me please

Or with every turn of the knob that makes my heart throb

For every time you entered my presence I was left robbed

Robbed of my innocence

Robbed of my choice

Robbed of my pride

You took my voice

As more and more of my innocence is taken

As I lay here, balled up and bones aching

As the thoughts flood my mind and my mind start racing

How could this be happening to me?

Can someone please tell me how this could be?

What did I do?

No wait! What did I say,

To make things turn out this way?

I kept quiet, hoping that will make it all stop

But it seems the more quiet I was, the more beatings I got

They quieter I became,

I started to feel less and less sane

But see, somehow, I thought silence was my friend

I thought silence was with me till the end

But silence said it was all my fault

Silence said that I was a failure

Silence said that I should be ashamed

Silence said that I was to blame

Silence said stay, don't go

Silence said they will all know

I stuck with silence and what's left of me that I have to show?

You took all that I have and that wasn't my choice

Even though I said nothing, you still took my voice

But enough is enough and I'm tired of being tired

Too many sleepless nights and too many tears I cried

As I mustered up the strength to make my way up off the floor

I told myself, you're going to break through that door.

So, with each step I took, I got a bit of my voice back

Saying girl, don't quit, don't slack

You're closer to the finish line than you think

Just whatever you do

Don't let your voice shrink

So, minute by minute and hour by hour

I'm realizing it's my voice, where I still hold the power

No matter what comes my way, I'm just going to scream louder

Cause I'm breaking through the silence like a blossoming flower

The Love I Never Knew
I Had
Ally Chinski

I was like any young girl who loved to daydream about a life other than the one she had. I enjoyed going to a place that wasn't home. It was music that was my real escape – I loved the way music made me feel. I felt loved when I listened to music. It made me feel as if I was being wrapped in the arms of the beats while the words of the singer spoke directly to me. The music snatched my soul and devoured my entire being as it washed away the molestations, the rape, the beatings, the pain of abandonment, just all of it. If there wasn't a song that would take it away, I was going to dream and pretend it had.

I wanted to feel love, happiness, and peace. I guess it wasn't in the cards for my childhood, but maybe I would get it in my adulthood. I dreamt of meeting a man that would take me away from it all. I didn't just want to be loved but I needed to be seen and heard. I met a guy, we dated for a while, I became pregnant, and then I had a miscarriage at five months. She was my little girl. My heart was crushed. I did what I do best: bury myself into someone or something.

My relationship with my biological family has always been dysfunctional or non-existent. So, I learned to create my own family. My best friend, Tia, is my sister. She may not be blood but she's been with me through the mud and we still love one another. She was always my right hand. Tia's mom was a mother to me. My and my mother's relationship wasn't stable; we would talk every now and then, but not too often. My dad and I had our struggles but we always seemed to make it right. He was my biological rock. In my dysfunctional family, verbal abuse was our norm. I was called names and cursed out on a regular basis. It taught me to hide in the shadows of others or my own hidden fantasy.

I met someone new. He seemed nice enough. We dated for a little while. He moved in, shortly after I found out I was pregnant. My sister Tia came with me to my doctor and Lamaze classes. It had been three years since I was last pregnant and this time it was a boy. I finally had someone that I could love and who I knew would love me back unconditionally. It wouldn't be forced or pretend, just genuine love. One day, while at work, two detectives showed up and told me I needed to come to the police station. They didn't tell me why but I spoke to my manager and he allowed me to leave. When we arrived at the precinct, the two detectives informed me that my boyfriend was currently on parole for a previous charge. He had also committed 36 armed robberies. Then, to top it all off, he was married and was still with his wife. How was this possible when he was sleeping with me at night? He led two lives, while innocent people tended to lead one. They informed me that I was a suspect. He'd told them I was the assessor, that I'd helped him in all those robberies. I was sitting there thinking, "I'm in a movie right now." The only thing that saved me was my job – I was working every time he committed a crime.

Sometimes I wonder, what did I do to deserve all of this? Will I ever find a love that's mine? Will I ever find someone who will love me for me? I'm lost.

One day I met someone who made butterflies flutter in my stomach. He had this unique smile that made a tiny crease by his dark brown eyes. He stood 6ft tall. He listened to me and was filled with charisma. To me, he was this gentle giant who loved my son. Our first date was dinner at my house. He played with my son for the whole evening. Our second was Chucky Cheese with my son. We talked for hours on the phone. I loved the conversations we would have, listening to his raspy voice. I would tell him all about my fantasies. I finally felt safe.

He knew just what I wanted in life: stability, family, unconditional love. And, better yet, he wanted it too. I was no longer going to be a statistic – a single mother working two jobs and living in the projects. I was dodging bullets. I barely had any family or really strong ties to anyone, yet my fantasy had come true. I finally had the man of my dreams. I felt like God had heard all my prayers. I was going to live! I could finally breathe, even if it was just for a moment. All the nightmares would be decimated as I'd found the love that I'd always longed for. We were engaged within three months.

His mother took to me and my son quickly. They didn't want me living in the projects with my son, so he moved us in with his parents. I told him, "It was fine until we saved for our house." It felt good to have someone care about not just me but also my son. All I wanted was love and I felt he gave it to me. He knew I didn't have any biological family ties but his family was close knit. I wanted what I saw in my head and it looked like my fantasy was going to come true. I was devoted to building this family – or was it the fantasy I was building?

Either way, I was committed to making this work, so I buried myself in him and his family.

We all have some issues and I noticed that he had some depression. I thought that I could help him and he could help me with the life I'd always wanted. It wasn't long before I noticed it wasn't just depression and he actually had some very dark moments. He started verbally assaulting me. Actually, this started early on but I'd felt that it was okay, since I was used to being called names. I was going to be a wife. Once we were married, however, it didn't get better. It actually grew worse. The verbal abuse would become so abrupt that my son would wake up. He'd always drunk beer, but it went from 6-8 beers to a 30 pack, a bowl, and a shot. Still, he had a way of making me feel loved, so I accepted the behavior. What I didn't know was that I'd married a narcissist.

Sometimes you think you have the power to change someone. You don't. The only person you can change is you. I wish I'd known that then. I could have helped him if only he would have let me, we could have been the family we'd always wanted. He would get upset, then spit on me. This became as normal as the name calling. He didn't physically hit me, but I still wonder if it would have been better for him to hit me than spit on me, as if I was nothing. How disgusting this was, yet I still thought it would get better. Emotional and mental abuse took full force at this point. I had this fantasy family. Was I in denial of how bad it was? Possibly. Everything was my fault. There was nothing I could do that was good enough. How did I go sixteen years without having any idea that the man I once loved could turn into the biggest monster I'd ever encountered? It was easy: I latched onto what I longed for. I held onto the image of family and not becoming a statistic, of being a single mother with two children – because now I had a child with him.

See, being abused was the norm. I was used to that, but I wasn't used to being a wife and having a home. So, I stayed. We would argue, but so what? My parents argued. A little sweet-talk followed. It was like Dr. Jekyll and Mr. Hyde. So, I just buried myself in the shadows yet again. It was my fault, what could I do to make it better? He would blame me for his mistakes. I really thought I'd found the love I always gave. Instead, I was so blinded by my fantasy. I didn't realize he could never love me as I did him because he didn't love himself enough. He was more in love with what I did for him, the care and concern. I focused on making it look good so I wouldn't be that statistic or look like a woman who had failed. I buried myself into being a mother, a wife, a hard worker, a backbone for his family. I was involved in Pop Warner and all the school events. I lost the most important thing: me.

I started noticing how he would mistreat my oldest son. Once I gave birth to his "son" and with my oldest not being his biological son, the difference in treatment from one child to the other was overwhelming. So many of his family members and our mutual friends saw the difference. I needed to get out. I was used to being abused, but it was something different when I saw what he was trying to do to my children by pitting one child against the other. It was jarring; perhaps I needed to see that so I would awaken out of the fantasy I was living. I didn't care, it worked. I was scared and alone with two kids. I had no knowledge of what I would do, I just knew that I had to break the cycle of this toxic life we lived. I got out and am still fighting for my life back. Who would have thought that leaving a narcissist would be so hard? I found out quickly.

Since leaving my ex, my boys and I have started counseling. My boys are growing as best they can with the challenges that have been placed in their paths. It took me a lifetime to finally focus on myself and my healing. I went back to school at last. I got my GED and my associate's degree in business management at the same time. I completed my degree with a 4.0 GPA. I was on the President's List for every module since I enrolled, all while fighting for my children and my freedom. I started my own consulting business with Scentsy. I re-found my passion for writing and the love I hold for poetry. I learned how to enjoy my own company for the first time in my life. My oldest son graduated high school the same year I graduated college. He has a full life filled with love and friends. One of my many challenges to being free was learning to be single. I went from relationship to relationship but I've now been single since 2018. That has been the longest time I have ever been single, but I needed to heal. I needed to give myself the love that only I could give me. I never knew that my own love could feel this way.

I have dreams that are meant to be lived and heard. I learned the power of loving me, because no one else will love you more than you can. You can survive at your lowest and still rise from it. Know that every broken piece is placed there for a new chapter, filled with stories to tell. Trust your path and, once you're free, chase your dreams – no matter what they look like to others. The love I was looking for was already within me. There is no greatest love. If I could go back and tell my younger self anything, amongst the many, one of the biggest pieces of advice I would give would be, "You are your biggest lover. Don't ever lose you!"

MEET THE AUTHOR

Allyson Chinski was born and raised in the Capital District of Albany, New York. Her love for her children is what shines bright in her soul. Ally is a very independent, strong, genuine, and loving woman. She is compassionate and emotionally aware. Her goal is to impact as many lives as possible by speaking her truth. "Imperfectly perfect, uniquely Ally" is her motto. She has always been passionate about music, poetry, and writing. With one of her dreams being to become an author, she kept faith in her journey. Ally is now ready to share some of the ultimate vulnerable moments of her life with you in her first anthology. She has learned that every woman in this world has been played, embarrassed, or misled by someone they deeply loved! Love is dangerous – it will have you dealing with things you knew you were too good for! She said, "We've all been fooled, that doesn't make us foolish!"

CONNECT WITH HER:

allymoe24@gmail.com

Identity

Brandiez Saimone

Does my job define me? Do my gifts and talents determine my worth? Who am I without them? Who am I without the pain?

In 2018, I was laid off from my job. This triggered some really deep wounds for me and I was in a state of worry and confusion. I depended on this job, I paid my bills and planned future endeavors with my income. The trigger for me was rejection. As long as I can remember, no matter how good things seem in life, I'd always had a thought – "This will not last and something negative will happen." For some people it may just be the nature of the mortgage industry, as layoffs happen when rates increase, but for me it hit deeper. It mirrored the feeling I had about most of my friendships and relationships in general. The feeling that, no matter how much energy, time, or love I put in, it just never seemed to come back to me. I felt like a nobody, someone being tossed aside when there was nothing more to take from me. It was this pattern of putting my trust in everything other than God that led me to the questions, "Who am I? Does a job, people, or things define me?" I'd been in church for most of my life, but at this moment I needed one-on-one professional assistance.

I had a therapist before but I didn't stick with it because the sessions were very pricey. I remembered the question "who am I?" in therapy, but I was in so much emotional distress that, when I think about it now, I don't think I had the space to try to examine myself. I was surviving and that was my priority. It's funny, I heard so many people say to me through the years, "No matter what happens to you, you always get it together." I knew they meant it as a compliment, but I never took it that way because I knew what it meant for me to hold things together. It meant, by any means necessary. I would pretend everything was okay, hide behind the church, and help others so that what I needed to address in my heart would someday disappear. This was why I hadn't figured out who I was. Who had the time? Therapy opened the door for my self-examination. What led me to therapy was a process of elimination. I had friends and family and the church and I thought to myself, "All these years, I've been very unstable financially and emotionally. I think it's best to try someone professional." This was prompted because I'd started to develop physical symptoms – heart racing, shortness of breath, and many other symptoms. I knew it wasn't normal and these symptoms only occurred when things were very stressful for me. So, I started digging deeper to find out where this identity crisis had started.

I never had thoughts or insecurities about my appearance at all, but when I turned nine and auditioned for a Broadway play, I started paying attention to my appearance and personality. One of my most favorite things to do was sing and it was the only thing I just knew I could do right. Some said I was conceited, but I wasn't. I swelled with pride. I didn't think I was better than anyone but that I was definitely blessed with a gift. I didn't get all A's like my sisters, I wasn't as "pretty" as they were, but I could definitely sing. I emphasized it because that was the most beautiful feeling in the world to me, singing and learning about God. I was one of the six finalists out of one thousand kids that auditioned. I was on the front page in the left-hand corner of the Jersey Journal… and that's when I got a phone call. The call from my father. At this point, I knew I had a father but I'd never physically seen him or even spoken to him, so this was a pretty big deal. I was in my mom's room and she told me that he was on the phone. I can't remember the full conversation but I definitely remember him saying he was proud of me. I told my mom that he sounded like Elvis Presley. I never spoke to anyone about my true feelings in reference to that call, but in many ways, not hearing anything at all from him afterwards led me to question myself. I questioned why I was rejected, I wanted to know what was so wrong with me that he felt it was okay to not be in my life. The feelings of rejection caused me to question my worth. The phone call from my father showed me that I had to earn his love, because I had never spoken to him prior to that moment. I thought I had to please those around me in fear of rejection, leading me to sabotage myself so many times in my life. I self-sabotaged the second audition, which was my first recognized moment of self-sabotage.

I wasn't fully comprehending everything that was happening and I was terrified of what success could mean. Success, for me, meant I had to keep up this image of perfection for others to like me and hopefully never be rejected. I also remember feeling really small and insignificant at the second audition. I had to excuse myself and I barely remembered the key to sing in. I was embarrassed, but there was a sense of relief as well. The relief for me was that at least I didn't have to deal with the added responsibility of being perfect. I didn't have a very close relationship with my mom at the time, but I was incredibly close with my godparents and grandparents. They all moved to different states right when I was dealing with being rejected by my father. Those huge moments contributed to my feelings of rejection.

As a child who was immature in their thinking, I didn't process my feelings in a healthy way. I operated from a place of seeking validation from others and I always felt like I had to earn everyone's love. Attending church and hearing sermons about how you'll be damned to hell when you sin didn't help either. I wasn't fully understanding the love of God, but I was an expert in His punishment. In fact, when I did something that I felt was sinful, I would wait for my punishment to happen, I believe, most times, I punished myself. I thought that people leaving was a direct response to me not being worthy. Or maybe I was just that bad of a person that they wouldn't want to associate with me. I became friends with many older women throughout the years, looking for the mother figure I'd imagined. The pastors were similar to father figures and I looked to them to fill that void. Unfortunately, because I was looking at them through the lens of what I imagined or needed, I missed who they were at their core.

During my incredible journey in therapy, we discussed that earliest memory of rejection and how my feelings of unworthiness resulted in very unhealthy relationships and friendships throughout most of my life.

March 2020, after two years of therapy, I was finally getting down to the part of my healing, where I understood more about my triggers and how they started but I was in a very toxic relationship. Healing looks different for many people and I had wonderfully supportive friends, family, therapist, and ministry leaders that assisted me in my journey. The most beautiful wake-up call during my healing, which I knew was divine, was my 3-month-old daughter. The pandemic had just started, things were looking very uncertain, and I was beyond nervous about the state of the world. I had also just returned to work again after maternity leave without pay. I was in a relationship that served no purpose for me in any area of my life, I had no support, the bills were almost always paid by me, any emotional moments were downplayed as not being that serious, and the verbal and emotional abuse outweighed any of the physical moments - which were not many but still one too many. I take full responsibility for allowing myself to stay for longer than the expiration date. I was at a turning point. I hadn't mentally been in that relationship since before my child was conceived, but the fear of rejection and a possible physical altercation kept me from leaving. My ex drank often and he would say threatening things, so I tried to make it work. I complied or avoided confrontation, hoping everything would be peaceful, but that cost me my inner peace. But did I have the strength to fight for my inner peace? The unhealed version of myself held on to the person I met ten years earlier, as I believed that the person I'd first met would come back. God knew I needed to leave that relationship, so I found that extra boost of strength in my daughter's existence. At that moment, my daughter sparked so much for me. Strained relationships with my family started to mend and I felt a level of support from those relationships that I hadn't felt in a long time. I had so many moments where I felt so bad for leaving that I felt like a failure. I wanted to be married and working on my second child by now, but that wasn't the case. I'm grateful, however, because the weight that relationship caused was too heavy and I now feel free.

In spring of 2020, I started to attend the online ministry She's Awakened, which gave me yet another burst of divine order I needed. I had to be in a space of willingness, which remains to this day, so that I can grow within Christ. The delightful part is that I was able to attend these online prayer and bible study sessions with someone that was a life coach. I believe every ministry should have a coach or therapist that one on one time is so important, as it helps to know that someone is praying for you and willing to help you navigate traumatic moments. Everything I went through didn't feel good, but I now know that all worked out for my good. My previous relationship wasn't the greatest but my daughter is the best thing that has happened to me, besides my relationship with Christ. I now know that people's opinions of me and whether they show up for me doesn't matter, because I have the love of Christ! The agape love, He loves me even when I am in my mess. I do not have to become perfect for Him to love me. I did not earn it, but He loves me. I have trials and tribulations now, but I have peace in the midst of it all because I know that God loves me and I know that nothing I have done or will do will determine my worth. It's not easy and it takes effort on my part, but studying His word for myself, spending time in worship, and attending services among others that are seeking His Kingdom... All of it helps me believe in His unconditional love for me. Consistency is the key. I was consistently waiting and believing in the negative things in my life, but now I am consistently seeking God and the good things that He has for me! I am what God says I am and now I'm free to move in the purpose of God. My purpose is to give God glory!

MEET THE AUTHOR

Brandiez Saimone was born and raised in Jersey City, NJ, and currently resides in Central, VA. Brandiez, considers her faith and family to be most important to her. If she isn't spending time with her beautiful toddler daughter, she's writing, singing, and acting in plays with Sistagal Productions in Hopewell, VA. I'm excited for God to use my life to give Him all of the glory!

CONNECT WITH HER:

elshaddi88@gmail.com

Surviving or Thriving
Holly Noble

I REMEMBER A TIME WHEN I WAS A REASONABLY happy child and when all I knew were the experiences, people, and places I had lived. I had a family with parents who loved each other, brothers who were playmates and companions, and grandparents, aunts, uncles, and cousins to celebrate holidays and birthdays with. My dad went to work every day repairing telephone lines. Mom stayed home and kept the household running like some moms did at that time. I even had a dog and my favorite time of year was summer. There were so many idyllic childhood memories of extended family and friends being together to swim, fish, boat, pick berries, and play lots of games around tables at night or when it was rainy. These are precious memories of a childhood I adored.

I did well in school and had mostly motherly and grandmotherly-type teachers who nurtured me and helped me learn well. I think I was the kind of child and young person who was easy-going, accepting, kind, and open-minded, except maybe when it came to fights and arguments with my brothers! We always ended up having fun together not long afterwards.

I wanted to please people I cared about and mostly thought the best of them. I "knew" deep down that there was a God from an early age, even though I hadn't been to church very much or been given much knowledge of faith. When I heard faith in Jesus explained around age 12, I eagerly accepted God's invitation to love me. I saw potential in everyone and everything... and I had a strong desire to help people know and achieve that potential. By all appearances, I was thriving.

In reality, things weren't as perfect as I originally thought or remembered. I had been "taught" to hide negative emotions and experiences, and that is what I did. I agreed to do whatever others wanted, pushing my likes and needs aside. I made it a whole lifestyle. I knew my family loved me, but what I didn't always see clearly during childhood, or even many of my adult years, was that my family lacked emotional intelligence, healthy communication, and coping skills. In fact, we were riddled with good people who struggled with mental illness and addictions. Parents, grandparents, and many other family members had mild to serious problems with anxiety, depression, and other mental illnesses. I later learned that this pattern went back for generations. I recognized, eventually, that my family members had acquired many negative patterns of coping with these unknown issues, like addictions and unhealthy codependent behaviors. The more I healed and learned, the more I remembered these types of things from my childhood. Things that I had dismissed in my young brain as normal. It was all I knew. What I learned as an adult is that, with the right kind of support, knowledge, and treatment, there was great freedom from staying stuck in these patterns.

I began to notice a strain in my relationship with my mom in my teen years. I knew she loved me but, aside from affectionately written birthday cards and thoughtful personal gifts, I was beginning to recognize that she had difficulty communicating with me in meaningful ways, which I deeply longed for. At times, she tended to snap at me and became withdrawn or almost cold when I came into a room, even though often she had just been laughing and having great conversations with one of my friends, neighbors, or cousins who had dropped by. She "tried" to find things we could have in common, but it would only last a short time. She didn't seem to have to try with other people. My brothers seemed to get lots of affection and time laughing with her. She and my dad were openly affectionate and obviously in love after many years together. I began to believe that I was the problem. I buried my pain in the deepest place I could find inside myself. In the end, however, I knew that it resulted in the desperate search I unconsciously went on in most of my relationships with both men and women. I needed that love that my mom had withheld. I was desperate to feel worthy of my own mother's love, but it would take years to be able to recognize and articulate that. It was confusing to see my mom's generous and good-hearted character in most areas of her life, but to know that she was strained and silent with me, her only daughter. The belief that I was unworthy stunted and trapped me. I seemed pretty together and wise at a young age – and I was in many ways. But this was one of the underlying beliefs that kept me from truly thriving as a person.

I think what brought a lot of it to a head for me was the summer after I had turned 16. Mom hadn't been feeling well and was coughing a lot. Since she was a heavy smoker, the doctor dismissed her concerns as too much smoking. She was losing weight and stamina, so Dad took her to another caregiver who gave her some tests. They found the tumor, a rare cancer which was incurable. After an unsuccessful surgery and standard treatments, she and Dad chose to have her come home to be cared for until the end. It was August and I decided to quit my job as a youth camp counselor to help out at home. She died the following January. It had been her wish to not die in the hospital and, while we were all glad to honor her wish, it had been hard watching her fade away slowly. My dad, brothers, and I did all we could, but we didn't talk much about what we were all living through. Kind neighbors, Nana (my grandma), and my pastor would come by to bring food or visit a little, but none of them asked how we were doing emotionally. All I knew to do was push all the pain down. Sometimes I cried and prayed, but I didn't even have words to express real feelings, since that had never been part of my vocabulary. I didn't fully realize what I was grieving at the time. I would sit with Mom day after day, rubbing her back, watching TV with her, and mostly hoping she would speak to me or tell me that she loved me. Anything to know that I was important to her before she was gone. I just wanted to know if she would miss me, that she hoped for good things for my life. She never did say any of that, or much of anything else to me. As a deeply hurt and emotionally immature sixteen-year-old daughter, I had no capacity to say it to her first. This ended up torturing me as well. I knew, deep down, that she did indeed love me and did the best she could, but I can clearly see in retrospect that her own emotional turmoil and childhood beliefs and experiences kept her from thriving in her relationship with me. At the time, though, there was no relief from feelings of the loss of my mother's love.

At nineteen I married Bob, a good man with my mom's temperament. Things were pretty great for a few years. It's painful for me to think about how I eventually fell apart every time I perceived that he wasn't nurturing enough, or if he didn't constantly tell me that he loved me, or if he seemed aloof or quiet or needed some time to himself. I didn't know it at the time, but these expectations were unfair to him. I was incessantly looking for him to give me all the love, attention, and affection that my mother had not seemed able to give. The more I asked him for it (and, in certain ways, demanded it), the less he seemed able to give it to me. I was pushing him away but couldn't figure out why this was happening. I became even more desperate in the belief that he did not truly love me. Bob was also on his own journey into emotional maturity and health, but this was such a lie. It was mainly the effects of childhood trauma, but it would be years of suffering before both of us would know that this was our pattern... and that there was relief for the pain that seemed to rip us apart. We stayed together and, by God's grace, had a mixture of good times and really difficult ones.

I didn't know it, but I was becoming more anxious and depressed as each year passed. I had no clue what that would lead to. I desperately tried to be a good wife, mother, and person and I never gave up, knowing deep in my soul that there was a better plan for my life and my family. I knew that God's love was real; He had proven it to me since childhood, in so many instances. I could fill a book with small miracles He had sent my way. I sought out help in any ways I could, some good, some not so great.

As others might expect, my relationships with other women also suffered. One of God's gifts to me was that I had been very close with my grandmother, but the feeling of disconnection and rejection from my own mother made it very difficult to trust the intentions of most other women, unless they initiated and carried the friendship. Again, my unconscious childhood wounds dictated my actions.

Eventually, in the midst of raising my children, the pressures became too great and I fell into a deep clinical depression. I had to get help. Bob and I floundered our way through a process and system that our current culture had stereotyped as dangerous and a cause for alarm. There was no other choice. After consulting several doctors and trying several types of medication, which took months, I was finally able to speak with a psychiatrist who gave me the medical support I had needed for so long. He prescribed a new medication that helped within days. Within weeks, I was feeling better than I maybe ever had.

I also found a female therapist who helped me begin to make sense of my long years of struggle. Of course, because she was both a woman and a mental health professional, my fears and false beliefs about therapy and mental health kept me resistant. I remember how anxious I was about our first meeting. I worked myself up so much that I was too sick to go. When I did finally work up the courage, God sent me the most beautiful miracle! I was called into the therapy room, and I saw her. She was seated comfortably in a chair near the center of the room. I openly started weeping. She waited patiently for me to compose myself, until I was able to tell her that she looked amazingly like my mom. She had the same hair color, build, face shape, almost everything. Only this woman looked radiant, vibrant, content, peaceful – things I rarely saw on my mother's face. I had the strongest desire to sit down at her feet and put my head in her lap. I felt like I was home.

Over many months, maybe a year, she helped me to see my family's history and how these patterns of survival – through unwellness and pain, combined with a lack of emotional management tools or any medical care – had just passed dysfunction down from generation to generation. How relieved I felt to learn that it was nobody's fault! What a freeing revelation that was for me – it was not MY fault! It was not Bob's fault! It wasn't my mother's or father's or any other family member's fault! What was left for me were the questions, "Where do I go from here? What do I do to get better?" Layers upon layers of false beliefs and childhood memories needed to be peeled back "like an onion," as my therapist put it. It has taken me years of hard work with skilled therapists, medical professionals, and family and friends to peel off my layers, make amends, and grow forward into thriving as the person I had always known I wanted to be. I am beyond grateful to God for where He has brought me, as well as for how I have gotten here. I will keep going. I have all the courage and strength I need to thrive for the rest of my life.

Meet the Author

Holly Noble was born and raised in Manchester, NH. Having an innate desire to see all people reach their highest potential, her compassionate curiosity, combined with a deep faith and love for people of all ages, has led her to years of people-oriented work. Some of this work has been centered around mentoring and educating a variety of age groups on various topics, social work, and volunteering. She is passionate about learning, nature, and her family, and can often be found baking in her kitchen listening to podcasts related to all kinds of health and wellness.

Connect with her:

Hnoble1010@gmail.com

Just One More Push
A Poem By

Zanyah Banks

When you think of the word push, what comes to mind?

I know, for me, hearing "It's time to push" was a good sign.

See, that let me know the end was near,

But, in that moment, it also brought a wave of fear.

The fear of the pain, the uncertainty, and if I'd get it right.

It's something about not knowing that makes me put up a fight.

But right then, there was no time to think "Are you ready for this?"

I just have to push and push until that baby shifts.

See, there's a few things about pushing many of us don't like,

So we will fight to keep from pushing – and if you shove us, you can take a hike.

For me, I didn't like that sometimes pushing comes with certain timing,

I like to move to the beat of my own drum, I know a few of us have that in common.

Now let's go back to my first thoughts of the word.

See, at that moment, push was the only word that I heard.

I would stop, take a breath, and think "Sheesh, is it over yet?"

The pain is kicking my butt, Tears falling, I couldn't hold them back.

Now I knew I needed to push in order to get through,

And yes, I guess the pain I endured was needed too.

See, the pain will convince you not to give things another try.

Your losses will be your answer when everyone asks why.

You convinced yourself you had given it all you'd got,

All because the pain and pressure from pushing had convinced you to stop.

I remember thinking "God, please get me through this!"

And my momma lookin' down, saying, "Baby, you can do this."

Now both times the doctor said "A few more pushes and you're almost there!"

So I positioned myself to push harder, because my blessing was near

Now the doctor said "Listen and hear me clear:

If you push when I say push, it will leave little to no tear."

One would think, with all the pain I was going through,

That I had to come out all banged up and bruised.

But, when they said push, I pushed,

When they said stop, I stopped.

And then finally they said "A'ight, girl, give it all you got."

Now at this point, I'm tired,

And I don't know if I have anything left,

But I've come way too far to fold because of stress.

The voices around me said "Oh look, there's the hair!"

So again I'm reminded that my blessing is near,

I took a deep breath in and I closed my eyes,

Then I gave it one more push and out came my prize.

See, the path to here was far from easy,

And I knew ahead wasn't going to be breezy.

Pushing didn't start when I walked in that room,

It started the moment I heard "You're pregnant" – boy, I thought I was doomed

But every step was a push,

Every teardrop was a push,

Every heartache was a push,

And one thing I learned was if you push a thing hard enough,

Eventually it will need just one more push.

MEET THE AUTHOR

Zanyah was born in 1990 in Newark, NJ. She is the mother of two biological children and one bonus child. Zanyah's love for doing different forms of art started as a kid. She would watch different dance performances over and over until she finally had it. It was then that her creative juices started to flow. In her early teenage years Zanyah and her family moved to Upstate, NY for a change of scenery. She soon joined her school drill team, danced, and participated in a poetry competition. She currently works with an organization that helps teens and young adults understand their why, run a profitable business, market themselves and much more. Outside of writing poems and dancing, she also learned to sew garments, do hair, and the importance of healing. As Zanyah walks in her purpose, she uses her poetry and motivational speeches to help others on their healing journey. Whatever she does, she does it with purpose and in her own way.

CONNECT WITH HER:

zanyah_banks@yahoo.com
www.instagram.com/your_motivational_poet/

My Trigger Had Purpose
Julia J. Banks

I was young when I had my first child. I was pregnant at 16. He was born when I was 17 years old. Most of my life was spent as a parent. My mom struggled with addiction which resulted in me having to care for my siblings. As I think about it, I was a caretaker very early in life. I focused on the needs of my siblings and my mom, then when I had my children it was my siblings, my mom and my children. There was a point in time when it shifted and my focus was my children, my mom and my siblings. This was the natural order of things if you consider this natural.

So, the idea of being an empty nester was scary but exciting. If you are not familiar with the term "empty nester" it is a parent whose children have grown up and left home. These times can be hard on both parent and child. I was excited because I was dating this new guy, we will call him Cory, it made this experience less scary for me. I felt like I was in a really good place although it was filled with emotions because for the first time in my life I didn't have to focus on anyone else but me.

I am caught up a little bit in Cory. I am in a place at this point in my life where I want to be. This is how I am feeling. I didn't have men come to my home when my children were young. The first time a man came to my house, my daughter was in her first year of college. I can finally have a man come to my house without fear of my children being affected. I can prepare him dinner, we will have good sex, all is good. The bible says "many are the plans in a man's heart, but it is the LORD's purpose that prevails". That was my plan but it definitely wasn't God's. His plan was much bigger than what I had in mind. As things begin to unfold I saw things I didn't notice before.

You heard me say how my mom struggled with addiction, but I want you to know that growing up in addiction has a set of challenges that if you have not experienced, you do not understand. I was the eldest daughter of a parent who was addicted to substances. That meant the responsibility to figure things out was on me. I experienced sexual abuse at the hands of a family member. My mom's addiction meant her need for the drugs came first. So the trauma I experienced caused me to have severe low self-esteem. The fear I lived in every day that someone was going to knock on my door and tell me she was dead, I wouldn't wish that on my enemy. I remember being in high school but not able to focus because I was always nervous. My dad also had an addiction issue. It's just that my mom's addiction was to drugs and his addiction was to women. You may read this and think well her mothers addiction caused more damage because it was far worse, if you are, you would be wrong. I remember being very angry with my dad. I wasn't able to articulate what I felt but I was always angry with him and my behavior showed him. I would try to fight him in public. I really wanted to make him feel the way he made me feel. I know their addiction kept them from showing up for me in the way that I needed them. Addiction is all encompassing and it controls your life. It doesn't matter what type of addiction. A person who is addicted to the life of the streets is just as damaging to their children's psyche as someone who is addicted to church. If you don't believe me, ask someone who was raised in church but no longer attends.

We have these experiences that may or may not be traumatic but we move on in life because if not, we will end up stuck. We usually tell ourselves, to get over it and keep moving forward. So this is what I did. I raised my children and now they're grown and I am on my own. I am really into Cory. I love his style, he makes me laugh. We could talk about anything. Some things he does get on my nerves but it's cool it's not a deal breaker. He keeps his word. He makes me feel good about myself, no pressure. In the back of my mind every now and then I say to myself, oh he can get it. I was attracted to him. I enjoyed his company. Things are going really well. We had been dating for at least six months or longer by this time. Cory made plans for us to go out one night. That night, I was afraid that he wasn't going to come. "He's going to use this opportunity to ghost me" was the thought that ran through my head. So I said to myself, "Don't get dressed, this way you won't be disappointed if he doesn't show up." My heart was racing and I was starting to sweat. In that moment, I had to push past my anxiety and fear by reminding myself of who I knew Cory was and what I knew to be true to me. I had to tell myself that I was going to show up and be beautiful. That I was going to be confident and his friends were going to like me – but if they didn't, I was going to be okay and shine anyway. I talked until my heart stopped racing and peace came into my living room. He arrived and we had a beautiful evening. I enjoyed his friends and they enjoyed me. Most of all, Cory and I had a really good time. I showed up in confidence and assurance that I had a right to be there. I thought that experience was odd and out of the blue but it passed, so I moved on.

We continued to date and things seem to be going well. I remember Father's Day 2016 a few months after the anxiety experience, that is what I'm calling it. I was home sitting in a folding chair thinking about my dad. I don't know why I was sitting in this chair. I am not sure why it was there. The couch would have been much more comfortable. I am sitting in this cold, uncomfortable chair thinking about my dad. I am remembering things I now realize were suppressed. I am flooded with a tsunami of emotions. I couldn't stop the tears. At this moment, I am remembering my childhood and the times my dad would tell me he was coming to pick me up but wouldn't. I would pack my bags, sit in the window, and pray, with tears falling down my face as I waited. I remember asking God-please let him want to come see me. No matter how hard I prayed, he didn't come. This happened more often than not, so I learned to stop calling. Actually, I learned to stop expecting. As a little girl, I learned to adjust my feelings to accept what he gave me. I felt I was an inconvenience to him. So instead of fighting for what I wanted I just stopped trying and accepted that I wasn't good enough. Whatever he gave me was better than nothing at all. I can now see how this showed up in my relationships. The tears were falling down my face and the dots begin to connect.

As I think about this experience and what was happening to me the night I was preparing for my date, I realized I was being triggered.

*A "trigger" in psychology is a stimulus that causes a painful memory to resurface. A trigger can be any

sensory reminder of the traumatic event: a sound, sight, smell, physical sensation, or even a time of day or season.

I couldn't understand what was happening because Cory did what he said. He showed up when he said he would. He kept his word even if it made him uncomfortable. Although Cory was who he was, it didn't stop me from experiencing him through the pain of my own trauma. Cory was a man that I was waiting on. I was excited. And all of these things created the stimuli that caused me to experience a trigger. It took me back to the time when my dad said he was coming but didn't. I distinctly remember feeling like the little girl in the window.

That night could have turned out very differently had I allowed myself to take out on Cory what I was feeling, because it had nothing to do with him. This is what happens when we blame other people for what we feel, even when what we feel is internal.

> *When you don't know the root most of the time you will blame what's in front of you. When what is in front of you is actually shining the light on what's in you.*

Purpose is the reason for which something is done or created or for which something exists.

The trigger brought revelation. It revealed the place of my wound. The hidden trauma that was unhealed. I never paid much attention to my father's actions because at some point in my childhood between ages 10 or 11 years old I just shut down a part of myself that needed him. I just couldn't do it anymore. I learned how to be present and disconnect. I had to do this because he was inconsistent, and unknowingly I felt that I needed to protect myself. The unhealed trauma surfaced and it was now time for me to examine my heart and how my father's actions truly affected me. The trigger revealed how I had not only shut my heart off to my father, but also to men. It showed me how I brought the relationship with my father into every relationship I had with a man.

I can see how God had to awaken the pain that was hidden within me so I could be healed. There were many times when the pain came up but I didn't hone in on it. Rather, I just looked at what happened in the moment and focused on the people around me for making me feel this way. It was much deeper than the people around me.

The trigger brought direction. I now have a starting point to work on in the area of healing. I have a direction. It's not enough to want to be in a relationship. It's also necessary to heal in order to have healthy relationships. I now can go to therapy with this new found information and talk about my relationship with my father and work through how it has affected me. I am not shooting in the dark but I am going after the culprit and confronting the target head on. The trigger walked me into my healing like a parent walking their child into school on the first day.

The trigger helped me to connect the dots. I can now see why I would shy away from certain types of men. I can see why in my naive years I entered relationships with men that were inconsistent and emotionally detached. I was. I had a relationship with my father who was also emotionally detached. As challenging as it was to admit to myself, some of the men I dated were a reflection of what was in me.

The years of denying my pain also denied me of my healing. I no longer run or avoid my triggers. I talk about them and work through them. I understand that they have a purpose. I now help other women lovingly work through the pain of their trauma so they can also stop it from spreading and infecting their relationships with themselves, God, and others.

When you find yourself experiencing an emotional trigger, it's okay for you to feel what you feel. Step away if you can, give yourself some space. Acknowledge what you're feeling even to yourself. As you give yourself some space, think about what you're feeling and what made you feel this way. The key is not to be reactive but to respond. This may mean you need to have a conversation but have the conversation once you're in a better mood.

The trigger that night revealed layers of limiting beliefs and allowed me to connect pieces to the puzzle that was me. We are all complex human beings. Our experiences follow us into marriage, school, business, ministry, parenting, work, and leadership positions. If we do not stop and examine our own behaviors we may end up hurting people and continuing the cycle of harm.

My mom told me a story about how she and her twin sister used to run from bullies, until one day she stopped and told her sister she was tired of running. They dropped their school books, turned around, and fought back. They never had to fight those kids again. This is how we're going to deal with pain. We are going to stop running and drop our defense mechanisms, facing our pain head on so it doesn't sabotage other opportunities. You can give your pain purpose.

https://psychcentral.com/lib/what-is-a-trigger#what-is-a-trigger

MEET THE AUTHOR

Julia J Banks is a mother and grandmother who lives in Upstate New York and enjoys spending time with her family and friends. She is a survivor of childhood trauma, physical and sexual abuse. As a certified life coach, she helps women who are ready to reclaim their self-worth after trauma so they can triumph in relationships with the self, God, and others. She uses her skills and life experience to empower women to give life to their voices and share their stories. She believes that once the pain surfaces, then healing will come. As an advocate for mental health and domestic violence, she uses her time to mentor women, connect women to mental health resources, and hosts monthly community meetings-"Women Empowering Women Through Support" all in effort to give women a safe space to share, heal, and be empowered. Julia is available to speak to women and young girls.

ABANDONING THE FEAR OF
ABANDONMENT
PEYTON JOHNSON HARRISON

FEAR OF ABANDONMENT IS **THE OVERWHELMING worry that people close to you will leave**. Anyone can develop a fear of abandonment. It can be deeply rooted in a traumatic experience you had as a child or a distressing relationship in adulthood.

I grew up not knowing my father. Actually, let me clarify that: my mother didn't allow me to have access to my father. She was so hurt and angry with him that she didn't deem it necessary for me to have contact with him or for me to get to know him. Her excuse was that he was on drugs and that she didn't want me exposed to this: that was legitimate, right. But what about my extended family? What about my grandparents, aunts, uncles, and cousins? Didn't they matter? Not to my mother. She was angry with him, so she was angry with the entire family, too. I only have one active memory of my father. I was playing outside in front of the house at 199 Chadwick Avenue and my grandmother said: "Here comes your daddy coming down the street." I remember looking and seeing this tall, dark, and handsome man just strolling down the street. My grandmother said something to him to make him acknowledge me. He was happy and pleasant and he played with me for a few moments. He gave me some candy and told me he'd come back to see me. I watched him walk down Chadwick Avenue, never to see him ever again until we met at his casket.

I never thought very much about my father until I finished college. I wanted to see him and let him know that I'd made something of myself. But, in retrospect, why was I trying to validate anything about my life to him when he had no interest in me? I asked my mother if she could get in contact with him for me. My mother got in contact with his sister, Barbara, who shared his contact information. This is where I began my on-again, off-again relationship with my father. I began to seek him out again when my son was born. I realized that my son needed to know who his family was and where he came from-- so I found him again. I found out he was living in Maryland with his family. We would call, talk, and have conversations. I would always inquire about when we should plan a visit. I really wanted him to meet my son, Brandon, his grandson. My father would promise that we could plan a trip soon but those trips never came to fruition. Empty promises.

In 2009, I began my journey to find my father once again. It was always me trying to have a relationship with him. He never pursued me. I always pursued him. By this time, we had entered into the age of social media and I decided to give Facebook a go at finding him. I remembered that my father had a son named Omar, so I went looking for a brother to find my father. I found an Omar with my father's last name and I sent him a message. He lived in Atlanta, Georgia. It took a while, but I got a response – not from him but his wife. She told me she would share the information with him. When I finally spoke to him, I found out he was actually my cousin. I shared some information about myself to verify that his uncle was my biological father. As timing would have it, several of my family members were in Atlanta at his house for a family graduation. I was immediately inundated with cousins all trying to talk to me at once. I went from trying to find my father to finding extended family. It was nice and scary all at the same time.

But with all of the excitement of finding family, I was informed that my father was still in Maryland – but he was dying. This was the biggest gut punch of all time: I finally found him again and now he was dying. I started talking to God and said, "Really, God? Am I being punked? Is this really happening to me?" And I have to be honest, I was pissed. What type of cruel joke was this? Everyone was planning to go see my father in the hospital. All of my new cousins were vehemently urging me to go and see my father. And, because life is full of dichotomies, at the moment I wasn't sure I wanted to go and see him. Isn't it ironic? Here I was, chasing after this man for over 20-plus years yet at this moment I didn't want to see him. And not because I didn't care about him or have feelings for him. Rather, I was hesitant to go because I didn't want my last memory of him to be in the hospital on his deathbed. As I was talking to God and trying to grapple with the decision to go to Maryland, my father passed away. God was merciful and made the decision for me.

So, my son and I made the trek to Maryland for my father's funeral. It was one of the most difficult and surreal experiences I've ever had. Just a blur of family, conversations, and awkward fellowship. My cousins, Greg, Cynthia, and Shelby were the most welcoming. My father's wife was nice to me, but I got the impression that she just wanted it all to be over so she didn't have to deal with me. At some point we were having a conversation and she mentioned to me that my father always talked about wanting to have a daughter. I sat there, flabbergasted. I said, He had a daughter." What kind of crazy was she trying to sell me? Why would she say something like that to me? Was she grieving or was she just being mean? It was hard to gauge, especially since I really didn't know her or have a personal relationship with her. So, I did what I do best: I wrote about it. Not only did I write about it, I wrote that exact scene as the introduction to my play, Does Your House Have Lions? I needed to get it out of my head because keeping that type of hurt and trauma inside of me would make me bleed all over everyone I knew.

I never really thought about the impact of growing up without a father. I was raised by my mother and my grandmother. Those two women equipped me with everything I needed to thrive in this world. I didn't feel as though I had lost or missed anything by not having a father at all. Until I met my ex-husband. I met my ex-husband during the summer after I finished high school. We were both working at the post office and I recognized him during our orientation session. I remembered that his sister was in my fourth grade class at Quitman Elementary school. I introduced myself to him and we developed a quick friendship. We worked the overnight shift from 10:30pm-7:00am and he walked me home every morning for 10 weeks. We fell fast for one another, and he told me immediately that he was going to marry me. I thought he was crazy, because I was on my way to Spelman College and no one was going to get in the way of that. My degree and my education were the goal. However, he won me over and we started this four year long-distance relationship. One of things that endeared me to him was that he told me he was always going to take care of me. I was astounded. No man or male had ever taken care of me nor had any man vowed to do it. That was a new experience for me. Here was a 19-year-old telling me he loved me, that he wanted to marry me, and that he was always going to take care of me. I was all the way in. But, in retrospect, why was I all in? I was 18 years old. Did my father's absence have anything to do with my need to attach myself to the first man who said he loved me? Did I have underlying abandonment issues that I suppressed? The answer is an astounding yes. I entered into my marriage believing that love conquered all and that we were going to win in this love game. But, as fate would have it, it was not to be. My husband had expectations of me that I never knew about. He never discussed what he thought a "wife" should be or do in his eyes and all of the love we said we had for one another shattered into a million pieces. He cheated on me, got his mistress pregnant, and proceeded to tell me how horrible a wife I was. I promptly asked him to not come back and changed the locks on my doors. Not only was he abandoning me; he was blaming me. I was devastated. It felt like it was another unexpected blow. We divorced.

I did everything I could to keep from being here, yet here I was. I was scared. How was I going to raise my son alone? How was I going to do it all? I wanted my son to be okay. I had these bills and the man that once loved me now didn't. My world was rocked but I needed to keep it together for my son. I wanted him to grow up, to be whole and happy, not traumatized due to our divorce. I always promised myself that I wouldn't interfere with his relationship with his father, no matter what happened to us. My hurt was not going to be his hurt. I would encourage my son to call his dad, check up on him and see how he was doing during his teen years. It was important for me to encourage the relationship between my son and his father. He left the marriage, and he left me, but not his son. I made sure that my son was aware of that.

I remember being at work and hearing a voice say, "You do know that you can write a play?" I was like "Really?" And I sat down at the computer and wrote my first play in three weeks. Becoming a playwright has been therapy for me–a cathartic experience where I not only get to share my thoughts and feelings but also tell stories that uplift people out of their own pain. I found that there's healing in lifting others. I believe that theater has the ability to channel people into a fictitious world where they can lose themselves but which can also provide a change in consciousness. My motto for my production company is "spiritual growth through theater." I believe that all of my relationships and life experiences have allowed me to take the pain and disappointment that I have felt and turn them into five separate masterpieces of healing which I call plays. I wasn't going to let it make me bitter. Today, my ex and I are the best of friends. I feared abandonment. I experienced it, but then I rose from it.

So, sometimes you may get knocked down in life by father's who don't love you or value your presence in their lives. Your husband might cheat and leave you to raise your child alone. However, know that God is always there by your side, holding you up with His right hand of power. He is your vindicator, your friend. All things work together for good to those who love the Lord and who are called according to His purpose. You've got this!!!

MEET THE AUTHOR

Peyton J. Harrison is a native of Newark, New Jersey. She moved to Albany, NY, in 1990 and has resided here for the past 32 years. She is a proud alumnae of Spelman College in Atlanta, Georgia, where she received her Bachelor of Arts in Psychology. Ms. Harrison worked in the field of human services and higher education for 21 years and pivoted careers in 2006 to work in the field of public health in maternal child health and chronic disease self-management. Peyton J. Harrison is an inspiring African-American woman who has publicly shone her light into the art world for almost two decades. She has passion in her soul for inspirational awareness that is expressed through the many pieces she has written. These pieces are more than a dialogue. Ms. Harrison has been writing, producing, and directing inspirational plays for the Capital District since 2005.

CONNECT WITH HER:

peytonjharrisonproductions@gmail.com

www.facebook.com/peyton.j.harrison.5

God Has the Final Say

Teron Hughes

"I can't breathe, that's when I realized I was dying." My name is Teron Hughes. I was born on October 29, as a twin, and two months prematurely, which caused my organs to be underdeveloped. For the first few months of my life, the hospital was my home.

After two months, my mom was able to bring me home. My brother had come home a few weeks before and life started with my family. My mom found out I had severe asthma at the early age of three and it was rough for me. I wanted to play like my twin brother and other kids, but some days I was stuck in the house on a breathing machine or in the hospital. As I got older, we moved a lot and I was doing what I wanted to do. I wasn't taking my meds correctly and my medication wasn't being supervised by an adult all the time because my mom was on drugs. This led to me being free to do what I wanted. My home life was unstable. My mom was a drug addict, which had led to the instability in our lives. We always knew our mom loved us and wanted nothing but the best for both my brother and I, although her addiction made it difficult for her to provide the best for us. I remember being in and out of the hospital a lot because of my asthma.

At the age of 12, my life took a dramatic spiral. I remember that day so clearly: I was playing with my brother outside like usual when I started to wheeze. I ran into the house and tried to take my rescue inhaler but it wasn't working. I ran to tell my mom that my inhaler wasn't working while I struggled to breathe. She told me to "sit down and be calm," so I did. As time passed, she asked how I was feeling. I told her, "Mom, I feel worse." She immediately said, "Let's get in the car and go to the hospital." I replied, "Okay," and we got in the car. I felt so bad and I remember telling her, "I'm not going to make it." She stopped the car and called the ambulance. She tried to help me control my breathing by doing the breathing exercises we were shown by the doctors. I remember thinking the ambulance was taking a very long time to get to us.

When the EMTs finally arrived in the ambulance, the first thing they did was check my breathing and put me on oxygen. I remember being in the ambulance and not being scared. I knew I was in a safe place. I was really tired and wanted to sleep but I knew I had to stay awake. The EMTs were very reassuring and told me that I was doing good. I remember looking at my mom and her telling me I would be alright, that everything was okay. I remember the sirens going off and by the time we finally arrived at the hospital, it felt like I was suffocating. The nurses and doctors wheeled us to the intensive care unit. I was so unstable by that point that I couldn't hold on any longer. I was dying and I knew it. I told them I was going to sleep and I did. The doctors told my mom that both of my lungs had collapsed. It wasn't looking good for me. They weren't sure if I was going to live, but God had greater plans for my life. "For I know the plans I have for you, declares the Lord, plans to prosper you and not to harm you, plans to give you hope and a future." Jeremiah 29:11. My family were all praying for me. I didn't know this at 12 years old, but God's word is true.

I spent two months in the hospital – one month in the ICU and the other in the Critical Care Unit. Two months is a long time to be in the hospital for anyone, but for a 12-year-old kid, two months felt like eternity. I would always listen to the doctors and nurses talking and overheard the doctors say they were "amazed" that I'd made it this far considering the condition I was in when I arrived at the hospital. Thankfully, the doctors were able to stabilize me and treat my lungs. However, I had to learn to walk and feed myself all over again. It was frustrating and I was tired all the time learning to walk again. It made me sad. I cried some days, but I knew I couldn't give up. The doctors told my mom that, when I returned to school, I might not be the same kid. They were unsure if I would have developmental delays because of the damage my lungs had endured. After I got out of the hospital and went back to school, I surpassed all their original assumptions. I passed my classes even though I had to work harder in school. I went to summer school and asked my friends to help me with my schoolwork. I had a tutor in school to help with math and history. My teachers thought I would fail, but I passed middle school, graduated high school, went to cosmetology school, and then pursued an education in natural hair care. I made it. When others doubted me and said I wouldn't, I did through hard work and determination.

I knew that there was an existence of something higher than myself even at a very young age. I would have vivid dreams as a young child. I have always felt that God had a specific purpose for my life – and I know that God has a purpose for your life as well. I moved out of my mother's home due to her addiction and instability and I moved in with my cousins and aunts. I was scared. I didn't want to move. I loved my mom, but they wanted better for us. It was a hard decision and it was very emotional for me to leave my mom. My cousin was a God-fearing woman who took me in and started to teach me the word of God. I got saved and they baptized me. I remember going to the *No More Sheets* conference in Atlanta, Georgia, and seeing Prophetess Juanita Bynum. I fell in love with her and her life story. I began to listen to her and the anointing on her life is so powerful. I was touched by her story and her music. I would listen to her sermons every day when I could. I knew then that God had a plan for me. The more I listened to Juanita Bynum, the more clearly I began to hear from God. My dreams became clearer, too. That was how my faith started to grow, a spiritual growth that I began to cultivate in my teens. I started to stand on the scriptures like Psalms 118:17, which states, "I shall not die, but live: and shall declare the works of the Lord." I am an overcomer and I'm alive today to share my testimony.

I am not perfect by any means. I'm still growing and becoming the woman God has designed me to be but, like everyone else, I have my share of issues. We all fall short of the glory of God and I'm not exempt from that. I have dealt with depression and anxiety. It's hard at times, but God. For those of you that have dealt with anxiety, you know what it's like. I get fearful at times and want to take a step back from everyday situations. I worry a lot at times and I know that this fear hinders my calling. God is definitely doing a new thing in my life. There were times in my past where I would have let the anxiety and fear of sharing my testimony prohibit me from writing this chapter. However, God has other plans and this chapter is meant for someone who is dealing with anxiety, fear, and depression. You are not these disorders. I believe that, through these obstacles, God is growing my faith, character, wisdom, and gifts. I know He will do the same for you. We all have to go through something to get to our breakthrough.

I am a blessed woman of God. I am married to the love of my life, Timothy. We have been married for 15 years and together for almost 20 years. Proverbs 31 has always had a special place in my heart: "*A wife of noble character who can find? She is worth far more than rubies. Her husband has full confidence in her and lacks nothing of value. She brings him good, and not harm, all the days of her life.*" (Proverbs 31:10-11). We have three beautiful children, Timothy Jr., Timia, and Timeka. I own multiple businesses and we own our house and more. I love God, I love to worship, and I love to do liturgical dance. God has blessed me with many gifts and talents. As a young child, God gave me visions and dreams which continued to develop as my faith in God increased. I hear from God and, when He speaks, I am obedient and deliver, thus saith the Lord.

God also gifted me with the spirit of evangelism. I use my natural hair care business as a ministry. God sends all kinds of people my way and I am able to proclaim the goodness of Jesus and all that He's done for me while I'm doing their hair. I have met so many people who have impacted my life just as much as I've impacted theirs while they were in my chair. My hair care ministry started when I was young, around the age of 14. As I got older and started doing hair professionally, Jesus just kept showing up in my ministry. As my clients would tell me their stories, God would lead, guide, and direct how I responded and it just bloomed from there. My ministry flourished through the COVID-19 pandemic, at a time when others lost their businesses, homes, and, more importantly, loved ones. I am so grateful to God that He not only kept my family safe during COVID but that He sustained our ministries. God is truly an on-time God, "*who will never leave you nor forsake you*" (Deuteronomy 31:8).

I own a non-profit organization 5013c. This ministry was birthed before my mom transitioned to be with the Lord. This ministry is called Blessed Hands Ministries and was birthed because we lived in homeless shelters twice during my childhood. I was exposed to so many women and children when we lived in the homeless shelters, which is how this non-profit was formed. I experienced first-hand how women struggled to provide for their children while maintaining their drug habits. There were kids there going through the same situation. We were not alone. I grew up and knew that if families got the right help, they wouldn't have to go back to shelters. Our hope is that women get the mental help they need so they don't have to go back to a shelter. This is a family and friends ministry. My children are active members of this non-profit and are learning how to care and provide for others in need. We feed and clothe women and their children who are in need. We also donate household items such as cleaning supplies. We launched our organization in 2017 to help the homeless, as we wanted to do what the Lord says concerning the poor in Deuteronomy 15:11, "*For there will never cease to be poor in the land. Therefore, I command you, you shall open your hand wide to your brother, to the needy and the poor, in your land.*" We are feeding the lives of God's people everywhere we go.

He used all my pain and long suffering for my good. He birthed ministries, gifts, and talents out of what could have just been seen as trauma. God keeps on blessing me.

MEET THE AUTHOR

A beautician and owner of a non-profit organization and raised in Richmond, VA, Teron Hughes uses her gifts and platform to change the world. She is a wife and mother that wears many hats. If you are ever in Teron's presence, you can find her in a spirit of worship, because she knows that it changes the atmosphere. She is a high school and Richmond Technical Center graduate. When not using her hands to create masterpieces on her clients' heads, you can find her spending time with her family. She enjoys waking up before everyone else and taking peaceful walks in the park to start her day. Many obstacles have tried to shake her faith, but she decided to use them to propel her forward. Teron's smile has a way of sending healing to your soul and gives you a glimpse of the love that Christ has for everyone.

CONNECT WITH HER:

TeronHughes@gmail.com

Journaling: Let's take a journey of awakening

She's Awakened

WHAT ASPECTS OF THESE STORIES RESONATED WITH YOU?

_____
_____
_____
_____
_____
_____
_____
_____
_____
_____
_____
_____
_____
_____
_____
_____
_____
_____
_____
_____
_____
_____
_____
_____

She's Awakened

ONE OF THE WAYS WE CONNECT TO ONE ANOTHER IS
THROUGH OUR PAIN. WHAT WAS THE PAIN YOU FELT?

_____
_____
_____
_____
_____
_____
_____
_____
_____
_____
_____
_____
_____
_____
_____
_____
_____
_____
_____
_____
_____
_____

She's Awakened

WHAT ARE SOME OF THE BELIEFS YOU HAD THAT
MAY HAVE BEEN KEEPING YOU FROM MOVING FORWARD?

_____

_____

_____

_____

_____

_____

_____

_____

_____

_____

_____

_____

_____

_____

_____

_____

_____

_____

_____

_____

_____

_____

_____

She's Awakened

WHAT DO YOU DESIRE TO DO DIFFERENTLY IN YOUR LIFE SO
THAT YOU CAN MOVE FORWARD?

_____

_____

_____

_____

_____

_____

_____

_____

_____

_____

_____

_____

_____

_____

_____

_____

_____

_____

_____

_____

_____

_____

_____

_____

She's Awakened

ENVISION WHAT YOUR LIFE WOULD BE LIKE ONCE YOU
MADE THE SHIFT TO DO THINGS DIFFERENTLY?

_____

_____

_____

_____

_____

_____

_____

_____

_____

_____

_____

_____

_____

_____

_____

_____

_____

_____

_____

_____

_____

_____

She's Awakened

WHAT DOES GOD SAY ABOUT YOUR TRUTH
AND YOUR EXPERIENCE?

_____

_____

_____

_____

_____

_____

_____

_____

_____

_____

_____

_____

_____

_____

_____

_____

_____

_____

_____

_____

_____

_____

_____

_____

_____

She's Awakened

WHAT CAN YOU SAY ABOUT GOD'S GRACE IN YOUR LIFE?
HOW HAS GOD COVERED, PROTECTED, AND KEPT YOU?

_____
_____
_____
_____
_____
_____
_____
_____
_____
_____
_____
_____
_____
_____
_____
_____
_____
_____
_____
_____
_____
_____
_____

She's Awakened

REFRAME WHAT YOU BELIEVED AND PARTNER IT WITH
GOD'S GRACE AND HIS WORD. WHAT IS YOUR NEW TRUTH?

_____

_____

_____

_____

_____

_____

_____

_____

_____

_____

_____

_____

_____

_____

_____

_____

_____

_____

_____

_____

_____

_____

Next Steps

Now that you have journaled you may be ready to do some more work and are wondering what to do next. I would love to continue your journey with you and so I invite you to connect with me in a few ways so we can talk about how I can help you continue to move forward.

Email me directly at julia@shesawakened.com

Schedule an **Empower Me** call at https://Empowerme.as.me/

Made in United States
North Haven, CT
19 October 2022

25655303R00059